Happy Birthday to

D1739159

Good Books™

Intercourse, PA 17534
800/762-7171 • www.goodbks.com

Text by Lois Rock
Illustrations copyright © 2002 Gabriella Buckingham
Original edition published in English under the title
Now You Are 2 by Lion Publishing, plc, Oxford, England.
Copyright © Lion Publishing 2002.

North American edition published by Good Books, 2002.
All rights reserved.

NOW YOU ARE 2
Copyright © 2002 by Good Books, Intercourse, PA 17534
International Standard Book Number: 1-56148-395-8
Library of Congress Catalog Card Number: 2002024102

Printed and bound in Singapore.

Library of Congress Cataloging-in-Publication Data
Rock, Lois
  Now you are 2 / Lois Rock, Gabriella Buckingham.
    p. cm.
  Originally published: Oxford, England : Lion Pub., 2002.
  Summary: Two-year-olds spend their birthdays tapping their feet, jumping
in the mud, playing in the sand, washing, playing, and hiding.
  ISBN 1-56148-395-8
  [1. Birthdays--Fiction. 2. Toddlers--Fiction. 3. Stories in rhyme.][I. Title:
Now you are two. II. Buckingham, Gabriella. III. Title.
PZ8.3.R58615 Nm 2002
[E]--dc21   2002024102

Last year, little darling,
I would often carry you...

But now you climb and walk
and run, for this year

you are

2

Here's a birthday
message from
the golden shining sun:
welcome to another year
of happiness and fun.

Two little hands
that you can clap,

two little feet
that you can tap.

A person who is two
has a most amazing smile
and a most amazing voice
you can hear for half a mile.

Now you are old
enough to choose
all of the things
that come in twos:

two little socks
for two little feet,

two little shoes,
all nice and neat.

Make your mark
upon the mud,
jump in with
a great big thud.

Make your mark
upon the sand,
draw a picture
with your hand.

A duck says **QUACK.**
A cow says **MOO.**

What can you say
now that you're two...?

Can you say **OINK?**

Can you say BAA...?

Oh
What an
animal
you are!

There's a time for everything in a busy day:

time to wash, and time to eat, and time to run and play...

Time to go exploring and
time to come inside,
time to make a cozy den
where you can simply hide.

Teddy is ready
to sleep now.
Teddy is nodding
his head.
Teddy is ready,

so

Ready,

Steady,

GO!

Off to bed.